The Paul Brady Songbook

Wise Publications
part of The Music Sales Group
London/New York/Paris/Sydney/Copenhagen/Berlin/Madrid/Tokyo

Published by:
Wise Publications
8/9 Frith Street, London W1D 3JB, England.

Exclusive distributors:
Music Sales Limited
Distribution Centre, Newmarket Road,
Bury St. Edmunds Suffolk IP33 3YB, England.
Music Sales Pty Limited
120 Rothschild Avenue, Rosebery, NSW 2018, Australia.

Order No. AM91411
ISBN 0-7119-6062-3
This book © Copyright 2003 by Wise Publications.

Unauthorised reproduction of any part of this
publication by any means including photocopying
is an infringement of copyright.

Music arrangements by Derek Jones.
Music processed by Paul Ewers Music Design.

Photographer Lorna Fitzsimons.

Printed in the United Kingdom by
Caligraving Limited, Thetford, Norfolk.

www.musicsales.com

This publication is not authorised for sale
in the United States of America and/or Canada

Crazy Dreams 6
Dancer In The Fire 10
Follow On 15
The Hawana Way 18
Helpless Heart 24
The Homes Of Donegal 28
I Believe In Magic 36
The Island 44
I Will Be There 31
The Long Goodbye 47
Nobody Knows 52
Not The Only One 57
Nothing But The Same Old Story 62
Oh What A World 90
Paradise Is Here 68
Steal Your Heart Away 74
The World Is What You Make It 78
You're The One 84

Your Guarantee of Quality:

As publishers, we strive to produce every book
to the highest commercial standards.

The book has been carefully designed to minimise awkward
page turns and to make playing from it a real pleasure.

Particular care has been given to specifying
acid-free, neutral-sized paper made from pulps which
have not been elemental chlorine bleached.

This pulp is from farmed sustainable forests and
was produced with special regard for the environment.

Throughout, the printing and binding have been
planned to ensure a sturdy, attractive publication
which should give years of enjoyment.

If your copy fails to meet our high standards,
please inform us and we will gladly replace it.

2. You're tired of dreaming someone else's dreams
   When they really don't include you any longer
   Miles from home, you're sliding down with each day
   And you need a woman's love to make you stronger
   And lately you've been getting doubts
   A voice inside keeps calling out
   That someone else's dreams don't get you nowhere.

3. So shut the suitcase, kiss the year goodbye
   Don't let nobody stop you at the doorway
   And close the shutters on this empty room
   Where these crazy dreams come crawling to devour you
   And head on out across that line
   Where she's been waiting all this time
   And tell her that you want her there forever.

4. *(D.S.)* It's still two hours till this plane gets down
   Can hardly bear to wait another minute
   Your sweet loving babe is all that I need
   Darlin' it's been building up inside of me
   Tonight we'll go and paint this town
   We're gonna drink champagne, till we both fall down
   And we'll find some other crazy dream tomorrow.

Dancer In The Fire

Words & Music by Paul Brady.

© Copyright 1983 Hornall Brothers Music Limited.
All Rights Reserved. International Copyright Secured.

2. Come runnin' to me with your soul in your hand
   Like a child who knew no fear
   With such a need to be alive
   I was scared to get too near
   With such a need to be alive
   I was scared to get too near

(*D.S.*) 3. And now it's three years later
   You're still eager for the game
   But your eyes can't hide the times you tried
   To live too near the flame
   Your eyes can't hide the tears you cried
   When you got too near the flame

4. But to you it makes no difference
   How many times you fall
   For you've seen the freedom through the flame
   And you can't resist the call
   You've seen the freedom through the flame
   And you want to taste it all

*Chorus You burn so bright into the night
   A dancer in the fire
   I wish I had your nerve right now
   But I'm still scared to walk the wire
   Yes I'm still scared to walk the wire
   I'm still afraid to walk the wire*

Follow On

Words & Music by Paul Brady.

2. Days of beauty calling
   Vanish through a haze
   Trapped inside some spiral
   With no ending

   Still you bring me loving
   Free me with a touch
   Lead me out to greet
   The calm descending
   When all is said and done
   You are the only one

The Hawana Way
Words & Music by Paul Brady.

Verse 2
This power takes me from the place I belong
To where only the strong get through.
You got to keep on believing or you lose your way,
It slips right out of view.
Though there are days the light can flicker and fade,
Here in this place tonight a fire is burning.

3. I'd like to stay along with you
   And while away the night
   With fairy lore and tales of yore
   Beside the turf fire bright
   And then to see laid out for me
   A shake-down by the wall
   For there's rest for weary wanderers
   In the homes of Donegal

4. The time has come for me to go
   And bid you all adieu
   For the open highway calls me back
   To do these things I do
   But when I'm travelling far away
   Your friendship I'll recall
   And please God I'll soon return unto
   The homes of Donegal

I Will Be There

Words & Music by Paul Brady & John O'Kane.

I Believe In Magic

Words & Music by Paul Brady & Gary Nicholson.

© Copyright 2001 Hornall Brothers Music Limited (50%)/Copyright Control (50%).
All Rights Reserved. International Copyright Secured.

The Island

Words & Music by Paul Brady.

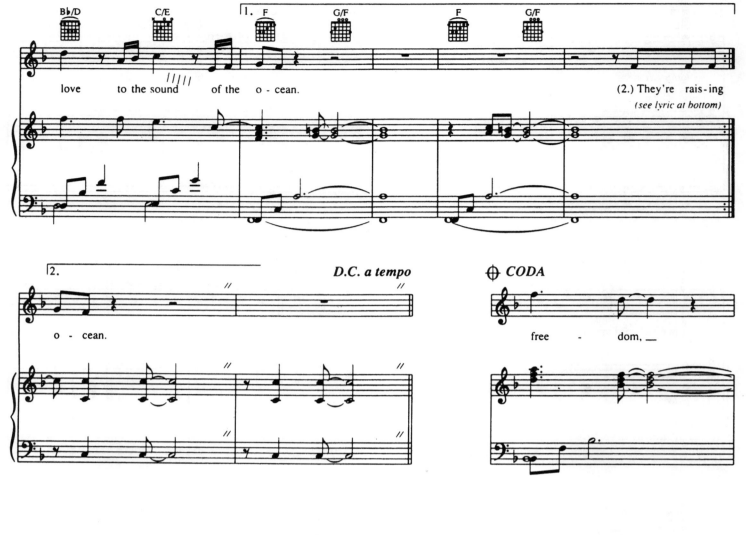

2. They're raising banners over by the markets
   Whitewashing slogans on the shipyard walls
   Witchdoctors praying for a mighty showdown
   No way our holy flag is gonna fall
   Up here we sacrifice our children
   To feed the worn-out dreams of yesterday
   And teach them dying will lead us into glory ...

3. Now I know us plain folks don't see all the story
   And I know this peace and love's just copping out
   And I guess these young boys dying in the ditches
   Is just what being free is all about
   And how this twisted wreckage down on Main Street
   Will bring us all together in the end
   And we'll go marching down the road to freedom ...
   Freedom

Nobody Knows

Words & Music by Paul Brady.

Not The Only One
Words & Music by Paul Brady.

Nothing But The Same Old Story
Words & Music by Paul Brady.

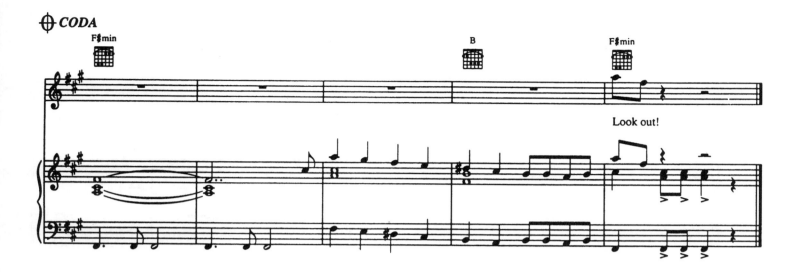

2. Came down to their city
   Where I worked for many's the year
   Built a hundred houses
   Must've pulled half a million pints of beer
   Living under suspicion
   Putting up with the hatred and fear in their eyes
   You can see that you're nothing but a murderer
   In their eyes, we're nothing but a bunch of murderers

(*D.S. 1.*) 3. I'm sick of watching them break up
   Every time some bird brain puts us down
   Making jokes on the radio
   Guess it helps them all drown out the sound
   Of the crumbling foundations
   Any fool can see the writing's on the wall
   But they just don't believe that it's happening

4. There's a crowd says I'm alright
   Say they like my turn of phrase
   Take me round to their parties
   Like some dressed-up monkey in a cage
   And I play my accordion
   Oh! but when the wine seeps through the façade
   It's nothing but the same old story
   Nothing but the same old story

(*D.S. 2.*) 5. Got a brother in Boston
   Says he'll send me on the fare
   Just wrote me a letter
   Makin' out that he's cleaning up out there
   Two cars in the driveway
   Summer house way down on the Cape
   And I know that he'd fix me up in the morning

6. I've been thinking about it
   But it seems so far to go
   People say in the winter
   You'd get lost underneath the snow
   And there's this girl from my home place
   We've been planning to move back and give it a try
   So I never got around to going
   That's why I never got around to going

Paradise Is Here

Words & Music by Paul Brady.

Steal Your Heart Away

Words & Music by Paul Brady.

2. I buy you diamonds, buy you golden rings,
   Buy you all kind of beautiful things;
   But that don't matter
   To a lover with a restless heart.

   'Cause you still wanna wake up to a different scene,
   Some screen gem like the one in your dream,
   And leave me standing like a fool in the wings
   Still waiting for a part to play.

Lyric on Coda

(2.) And maybe you feel that it's alright
   To leave me waiting every night,
   To put me down in company
   In front of everyone we see,
   To take my loving when it's free
   And then to throw it back at me,
   Well baby I just can't stand it.

(3.) 'Cause I can be the one for you
   And I can make your dream come true,
   And I can love you like he can
   'Cause fancy clothes don't make no man
   Believe me baby
   I got what it takes
   To make you feel good.

(4.) And maybe you think a man
   Should be as perfect as a man can be
   To love you when you're feeling down
   And miss you when you're not around
   Well I can't be that one for you,
   I can only be the one
   That loves you.

(5.) Oh,
   What's this on your mind?
   Oh,
   What's this change of mind?
   Oh,
   What's this on your mind?
   Oh. **Ad lib. to fade**